THEY DIED TOO YOUNG

FREDDIE MERCURY

BY
Simon Boyce

D1433227

This edition first published by Parragon Books Ltd 1995

Produced by
Magpie Books Ltd, London

Copyright © Parragon Book Service Ltd 1995
Unit 13–17, Avonbridge Trading Estate, Atlantic Road
Avonmouth, Bristol, BS11 9QD

Illustrations courtesy of: Rex Features

ISBN 0 75251 105 X

A copy of the British Library Cataloguing in Publication
Data is available from the British Library.

Typeset by Hewer Text Composition Services, Edinburgh
Printed in Singapore by Printlink International Co.

FREDDIE MERCURY

In 1975, the music world was turned upside down by the release of the single 'Bohemian Rhapsody' by the monster rock band Queen. 'Bo-Rap', as it became known, was unlike anything rock had heard – or seen – before. The song was a canival-like fusion of over-the-top opera and grinding heavy rock. The vocals included fantastically complex harmonies, with the voices of 180 singers blending in the operatic choruses. At six minutes long, it was more than twice as long as the average single.

'Bohemian Rhapsody' shot to number 1 in the pop charts. And it stayed there for nine weeks – a record that held until 1991. Within three months of its release the single had sold a million copies in the UK alone. To this day it is one of the most popular rock songs ever recorded.

And 'Bohemian Rhapsody' was a sensation for another reason too. The song marks the beginning of the pop video. When the band couldn't get a slot on the British music show *Top of the Pops*, they decided to send in a film that could be shown while the track was playing. They commissioned director Bruce Gowers to put the film together. It cost £5,000. That's not a lot by today's standards: the video for Michael Jackson's 'Black and White' cost £4 million. In 1975, however, £5,000 was a substantial outlay. But it was worth it. The video stunned audiences with its special-effects images of the band members, heads zooming around the screen and breaking up into multi-coloured patterns.

Only one man could have created a single and a video as outrageous and theatrical as 'Bohemian Rhapsody'. The song was written by Queen's lead singer, Freddie Mercury, the greatest showman in the history of rock. Freddie Mercury was a flamboyant superstar. His peformances on stage were wildy camp, theatrical extravaganzas. And off-stage his life was as wild and operatic as a performance of 'Bohemian Rhapsody'.

Exotic Beginnings

The king of Queen was born Farookh Bulsara on 5 September 1946. His birthplace was the island of Zanzibar, a tropical paradise off the East coast of Africa, famed for its exotic spices. It was a suitable beginning for the man who would become one of the most exotic of singers, and whose life was spiced with sex and excess.

His parents were Persian. His father Bomi was a civil servant, a clerk in the island's judiciary. Freddie got his first taste of stardom at the tender age of one. A local photographer snapped a picture of the toddler, which promptly won first prize in a beautiful baby contest. In the afternoons, as Farookh grew up, his devoted parents would take him to play on Zanzibar's miles of golden beaches, or perhaps to the gardens of the Zanzibar museum. At night, they would read to the young boy. One of his favourite bedtime stories was *The Arabian Nights*. The heroes and heroines of the fabulous tales were Persian, like him, and their adventures appealed to his young imagination.

When Farookh was 8, he was sent to school in Bombay. He attended St Peter's English boarding school just outside the city. His school friends there christened him Freddie, a name which his family also adopted. Although St Peter's was thousands of miles from the English shires, the school aimed to give its pupils a traditional English public school education, and that meant lots of typical public school sports. 'I loathed cricket and long-distance running', Freddie remembered. 'I was completely useless at both. But I could sprint, I was good at hockey, and I was just brilliant in the boxing ring, believe it or not!' Boxing was a strange talent for the man who would become one of rock's campest stars. And his mother disapproved. She wrote to Freddie telling him to stop boxing because it was too violent. Instead, he focused on table tennis, becoming the school champion in the fast and furious sport at the age of ten.

But Freddie was not just a sportsman. At age twelve he was awarded the school's trophy for best Junior All-Rounder. Among his other talents were art and, of course, music. He was always sketching and painting. And he began taking piano lessons, and joined the choir. It was Freddie's mother who made him keep up his lessons. 'I took piano lessons at school and really enjoyed it', he says. 'That was my mother's doing. She made sure I stuck at it. At first I kept up lessons because I knew she wanted me to, but then I really loved playing.' Soon, he formed his first band, The Hectics, which played at school dances and fêtes. He also began to develop the theatrical style that would make him such a great performer by taking part in school theatre productions.

At school he was exposed to a heady mixture of musical styles. Most of the time he would listen to mystical Indian music. But he would also listen avidly to his parents' collection of classical music, especially opera, as well as a smattering of the rock and roll that was beginning to take the West by storm. The influence of this cocktail of styles was to be evident in the intricate compositions Freddie would later pen for Queen.

The Bulsaras were Zoroastrians, followers of the prophet Zoroaster. He had taught that celibacy and abstinence sap man's spirit and make him susceptible to evil.

Certainly, Freddie seemed to live out the principles of Zoroastrianism in later life. He lived life to the absolute hilt, spurning celibacy and living to excess. He became a full member of the religion at age eight, in the solemn Navjote ceremony. In front of eternal fires he repeated the appropriate prayers, accepting the teachings of the religion as revealed to Zoroaster by the god Ahura Mazda. He was given a shirt known as a *sudreh*, made out of white muslin to symbolize purity. The high priest tied around his waste a *kusti*, a cord woven from purest white wool. The young initiate was showered with rose petals, coconut shavings and pomegranate seeds.

From Zanzibar to Feltham

For Freddie, those school days in Bombay were some of the happiest of his life. Not only was he successful and fulfilled at school, when he was at home there were servants to feed him, lay out his clothes, and attend to his every need. After finishing at St Peter's he went back to his family's flat in Zanzibar. But when he was eighteen he was uprooted again. In 1964, Zanzibar's African majority launched a revolution against the minority

Arab rulers. The Bulsaras fled the violence and turmoil and ended up in England. They made their new home in the London suburb of Feltham, in Middlesex, in a semi-detached home smack in the flight-path for London's Heathrow Airport. His parents would stay in that house even when Freddie became a superstar; he could never persuade them to let him buy them another home. For Freddie, the grey and drab Feltham was a far cry from the exotic lands of his youth. But 1964 was an exciting time in Britain. The swinging '60s were under way. Angry, exciting pop groups were emerging, and Freddie began to get caught up in this new and groovy world.

Freddie had always enjoyed art, and in 1966 he began to attend Ealing art

Freddie Mercury

Queen on stage at the time of 'Bohemian Rhapsody'

school. The school was something of a hotbed of musical talent. The Who's guitarist Pete Townshend had studied art there, as did Rolling Stone Ron Wood. Freddie found himself coming under the influence of the burgeoning music scene. His classmates remember the kid with the goofy teeth grabbing his ruler or set-square and using it as a pretend guitar while he sang Jimi Hendrix songs. Freddie had become obsessed by the American blues guitarist. Again and again he would draw and paint the wild rock star, who had made his home in London. Later in life he would say that his two greatest influences were Jimi Hendrix and Liza Minelli. But his fellow students couldn't yet see the future superstar in the skinny youth miming with his fake guitar. Says film director

Graham Collis, who also went to Ealing: 'He was quite wet and used to giggle like a schoolgirl. We didn't think he was particularly talented. When he used to stand up and mimic Jimi Hendrix we used to shout him down saying "Sit down Freddie, you'll never be a success".' And indeed, he was relatively quiet and unassuming in those days. Freddie Bulsara had yet to become Freddie Mercury.

The Crowning of Queen

But that was soon to change. In 1968, a physics student at London University's Imperial College, Brian May, teamed up with a former dentistry student named Roger Taylor and art student Tim Staffell to form the group Smile. Staffell was a fellow student of Freddie's at Ealing. The two of them and another colleague would spend their afternoons practising singing three-part harmonies in the college toilets. Staffell started taking Freddie along to Smile gigs, and he soon became a real groupie of the band. He would travel to gigs in the band's van. And the others noted a strange thing about their number 1 fan. No matter how far he went, cramped in among the amplifiers and the drum kit, he would always emerge immaculate, his white satin trousers pristine. He was a great admirer of May's guitar playing, and he got on well with both May and Roger Taylor. He also realized that he desperately wanted to be in a band of his own.

In 1969 he was introduced to a group called Ibex and began singing for them. Ibex's manager, Ken Testi, remembers the audition. 'We auditioned Freddie to take over lead vocals . . . We were all competent players, but none of us could sing. Freddie had a great voice, with a terrific range, but he didn't really know how to use it. Once we had Freddie, we were a little rough and ready, but we showed a lot of potential.' It was while playing with Ibex that Freddie began to work on his stage act. Sometimes he would get a little carried away. 'We used to yell at him, "For goodness sake Freddie, just stand still!!",' recalls guitarist Mike Berstin. 'He was all over the place, such energy, but it wasn't done then.'

Ibex travelled up and down the country playing gigs in schools, colleges and pubs. Freddie was already beginning to adopt the outrageous clothes that would be his trade mark in later life. He was also a fastidious dresser. At one gig he was wearing skin-tight satin trousers, and he spent half an hour in front of a mirror before the show straightening the seams. But Ibex were going nowhere fast. For a start they were making almost no money. They'd make about £25 a gig. And £15 of that would go on the lighting show. The rest of the band wondered whether the lights were worth it. But Freddie, the showman, wouldn't consider going on without them.

Their last gig was a disastrous performance at the Wade Deacon Grammar School for Girls in Widnes. The sound was awful and the equipment didn't work properly. Freddie was using an ancient mike stand with a huge heavy base. At one point he tried to swing it round in one of his theatrical gestures and the base fell off. But Freddie carried on singing using just the pole. From then on, his mike stands would never have a base. And he would put this to good advanage, using the pole as a fake guitar, as he had used his ruler back in the days at Ealing art school.

But that was the end of Ibex. For a while Freddie sang with a group called Sour Milk Sea, and when they broke up he set up his own band, Wreckage. That too didn't last long. However, Freddie was still hanging out with the members of Smile. Many of them lived together in various flats around London. Ibex drummer Mick Smith remembers that Freddie had an early morning routine. 'Most mornings Freddie would be up first. He had a white Fender Telecaster guitar and he would walk around the flat, stepping over the various bodies still trying to get some sleep, strumming and singing the Who's "Tommy". It was quite a ritual.

They did the usual things – partied, smoked grass. Freddie himself recalls one occasion when Ibex bassist John Taylor made some hash cakes. 'At about midnight the police came, some kill-joy neighbour had called them. We invited them in, and gave them a drink and a couple of these cakes. We all fell about, but they left not knowing a thing. I would love to have been a fly on the windscreen of their police car after about half an hour when the effects of the dope hit them.'

The famous white leotard

Queen at the height of their fame

Freddie was spending more and more time with Smile's drummer, Roger Taylor. He and Roger had opened a stall in the hip Kensington market. They started flogging paintings contributed by friends, but soon decided that selling clothes would make more money. They had plenty of contacts and managed to get hold of Victorian clothes, furs, hats and other items. On one occasion Roger sold Freddie's own jacket after a customer saw it hanging up and took a liking to it. He got £20 for it, but Freddie, furious, rushed after the customer, returned his money and demanded the jacket back. He threatened Roger with violence. But Roger said he'd only sold it so they could get something to eat and a taxi home. When Freddie's hero Jimi Hendrix died, they closed the store for the day as a mark of respect.

Smile were once described as 'the loudest group in the Western world'. But they only released one single and that was a flop. When Tim Staffell decided the group was a dead end and pulled out, Freddie stepped in to take his place. And so it was that in April 1970 the band that would be Queen came into being. In 1971 the Queen line-up was completed when John Deacon joined on bass.

Queen Rule the World

The name 'Queen' was Freddie's idea. Brian thought it was too camp. But Freddie insisted. 'It's just a name', he said. 'But it's very regal, obviously, and it sounds splendid. It's a strong name, very universal and immediate.' He felt that the connotations of pomp and circumstance that the name conjured up were perfect for the kind of act that Queen would be. He also decided that *he* needed a new name, and Freddie Bulsara became Freddie Mercury. Mercury was the mythical messenger of the Roman gods, and Freddie must have believed that his songs would have divine inspiration. A lot of Queen fans would agree with him.

Freddie also came up with a logo for the group. He based his design on the four band members' birth signs. Brian was a Cancer, Roger and John both Leos, and Freddie was a Virgo. So his finished logo featured two lions holding up a 'Q' around a crown. There was a crab on top and two fairies (for Virgo) playing at the bottom. Rising behind it all was a phoenix – symbol perhaps of Queen's success rising out of the ashes of Ibex, Smile, Sour Milk Sea and Wreckage.

It took the new group a while to get going. They did the usual round of gigs in colleges, pubs and clubs around the country. And then, in 1972, they were talent-spotted by executives from Trident Audio Productions, who managed to swing a deal with record industry giant EMI.

The band looked like no other band out there. Standard garb at that time was jeans and T-shirts. But when Queen strutted on to stage they did so in silk costumes, dripping with jewllery. They began to paint their fingernails black. And black-and-white became a theme for the band. They also began to build up a loyal following of groupies.

The group's debut single, 'Keep Your-self Alive', flopped. So did their first album, *Queen*. The *New Musical Express*'s Nick Kent called it 'a bucket of urine'. Their second album, *Queen II*, did better, and pulled sales of the first LP up with it.

Queen began to trail around to record companies trying to get a decent contract. But their first real success came in 1974, with 'Seven Seas of Rhye'. And from then on Queen never looked back. The album *Sheer Heart Attack* and the classic single off it, 'Killer Queen', were huge hits. And then came the phenomenon of 'Bohemian Rhapsody'.

Incidentally, 'Bohemian Rhapsody' almost didn't make it as a single. Its weird

Freddie camps it up for a Queen video

The new-look Freddie on stage with
Brian May

mix of musical styles, and the fact that it was so long, made executives at EMI very nervous. Not only would it bore rock fans, they believed, but no radio station was going to play a single that was six minutes long. Or so they thought. But the band refused to cut the song. Said Freddie Mercury: 'We were adamant that "Bohemian Rhapsody" could be a hit in its entirety. We are willing to compromise in many things, but butchering a song is not one of them.' Then DJ Kenny Everett got hold of a copy of the single before it was released. Everett wasn't supposed to play the song on air. But he loved it and he was certain the public would love it as well. He played it whenever he could, creating so much demand for the single that EMI was forced to release it.

Freddie never revealed what the strange lyrics of the song meant. He only said that its meaning was personal, and that the song was about relationships.

'Bohemian Rhapsody' was released on an album called *A Night at the Opera*. At the time, it was the most expensive album ever made. It also featured a version of the National Anthem. When that track was played at the press launch, Freddie insisted that everyone stand to attention.

Queen later released another LP called *A Day at the Races*. Both titles were taken from classic movies by the comic geniuses the Marx Brothers. Queen had to write to Groucho Marx to ask for his permission to use the movie titles.

Groucho replied: 'I am very pleased you have named one of your albums after my film and that you are being successful. I would be very happy for you to call your next one after my latest film, The Greatest Hits of the Rolling Stones.'

After 'Bohemian Rhapsody', Queen were rock royalty. The group recorded an average of one LP a year from 1973 to 1991. They began to play bigger and bigger venues, and in fact are credited with the invention of 'stadium rock'. They won numerous awards and sold millions of albums. The critics were often harsh to Queen, dismissing them as a glam rock version of Led Zeppelin. But the band built up a following of millions of fans around the world.

The King of Queen

Of course, Freddie Mercury can take much of the credit for making Queen the band they were. He wrote many of the group's smash hits. He composed the awesomely successful 'Bohemian Rhapsody'. He was responsible for the stadium rock classic 'We Are the Champions'; it became a huge hit in the United States and was adopted by the New York Yankees baseball team as its anthem. He was also the composer of the disco hit 'Another One Bites the Dust'. This was Queen's greatest 'cross-over' hit. It was picked up by a black music station in New York City, who apparently thought Queen were a black act. Either way, the station got an enormous response from its audience, and other stations began to play the single. In the end, the song went to number 1 in the USA, and stayed there for five weeks. During the Gulf War against Iraq, 'Another One Bites the Dust' was the most requested song on Gulf Forces radio. And after Iraq had been defeated, 'We Are the Champions' took over. One record company even released a special very limited edition CD to the armed forces. It features then-President George Bush's victory speech together with 'We Are the Champions'.

But more important than his contribution to the band's music, Freddie Mercury was the focus of the band's live show. Brian May and John Deacon were quite shy men and Roger Taylor was hidden behind his drums. So it fell to Freddie to act as the band's showman. It was a role he relished and performed with gusto. He would appear on stage dressed in outrageously revealing costumes. He would wear white or silver leotards and catsuits, velvet trousers, hot pant shorts, tights, leather jackets. Always, his thick chest hair would be prominently displayed. Later on, he got into leather. The lead singer of the heavy metal band Judas Priest, Rob Halford, decided that Freddie had to prove he was manly enough to wear all this leather. So Halford challenged the Queen singer to a race around Brands Hatch racing circuit on huge motorbikes. Freddie said he would accept the challenge on condition that Halford dance with the Royal Ballet first, as he once had. Strangely, Halford dropped his leather challenge.

Part of Freddie's leather outfit was blue or red knee pads which he would wear over red or black leather trousers. When the band played the Liverpool Empire Freddie wore one red and one blue knee pad – to keep both the Liverpool and the Everton supporters happy.

The Showman

Freddie loved to be up on stage in front of thousands of fans. He would strut about, swinging his baseless mike stand wildly, or playing it madly like a guitar. He had a range of characteristic poses that were distinctively Freddie Mercury. He would stand at the front of the stage, arms akimbo, his legs spread, his head cocked to one side. He would prance about as though he was dancing his own ballet. He was a charismatic man. And as he sang his way through happiness, love, pain, depression, so the audience would be pulled along with him on his emotional rollercoaster. David Bowie once said of them that 'he was a star who could hold the audience in the palm of his hand'. At Queen's famous gig in Rio de Janeiro in Brazil in 1985 almost everyone in the crowd of 325,000 joined him to sing 'Love of My Life'. In Mannheim, Germany, he conducted with his short mike stand, waving it like a royal sceptre as 80,000 Germans sang a lusty version of the *British* National Anthem.

In September 1975, Queen performed at a free outdoor concert in London's Hyde Park. It remains the biggest concert ever held in the Park – as many as

200,000 fans turned up to see the gig. Freddie was his usual spectacular self. He appeared in a custom-made skin-tight white leotard. Half-way through, he exchanged it for an identical black one with a diamante-studded crotch. When the gig was over, the crowd refused to leave. They whistled and stamped and demanded an encore. However, Queen were under strict orders from the police not to go back on stage. Freddie was furious at not being able to return to give the scream-ing crowd an encore. But the police said they would arrest him if he tried it. He thought about doing it anyway, but realized that being thrown into jail in tights and a leotard was probably not a good idea, and he gave in.

The 1985 concert in Rio

The King of Queen

At the last gig of their 1977 USA tour a huge Father Christmas appeared on the stage, bearing an oversized bag of gifts – out of which leapt . . . Freddie. A Christmas treat for Queen's fans.

Freddie had always loved ballet. He was a special fan of the Royal Ballet, and a close friend of Wayne Eagling, one of the principal dancers. When the Royal Ballet was organizing a special performance to raise money for mentally handicapped children, Freddie was approached to see if he would join the dancers in a piece to be choreographed by Eagling.

He began a regime of exercises and stretching. He decided to perform 'Bohemian Rhapsody' and a new song called 'Crazy Little Thing Called Love'. Both would be played by an orchestra, with Freddie singing. Although Freddie had never done any ballet dancing, the performance was a resounding success. The audience, which was full of ballet connoisseurs, give him a standing ovation.

Freddie was famous in the rock world for his showmanship and posing. Queen was one of the highlights of the biggest concert ever – the Live Aid show that singer Bob Geldof arranged in 1985 to raise money for famine relief. After the show Geldof described Queen as the biggest band on the planet. And he pointed out that the event had been the perfect stage for Freddie, who was able to pose in front of the whole world.

In 1980, Freddie changed his image. He had realized that he was homosexual and decided to adopt a gay 'look'. He cut his flowing black hair, much to the grief of many of his female fans. He grew a macho moustache, and stopped painting his fingernails. As a result the band's offices were flooded with gifts of razor blades and nail polish. And at the first gig of that year's North American tour, in Vancouver, Canada, the audience bombarded the stage with disposable razors.

Star of Stage and Screen

Freddie's artistic sense meant that he always made a key contribution to the band's videos. For Freddie, the promotional films were a way of taking the showmanship and theatricality he displayed on stage into a new dimension. He loved to dress up and play different characters, and the videos gave him the opportunity to ham it up in front of the cameras. But he also appreciated the importance of a good video to the

Freddie Mercury with Boy George

Singing 'Barcelona' with Montserrat Caballe

success of a single. 'We realized earlier on there was a different way to sell records and now video has become an integral part of making music', he pointed out. 'When you release a single it conjures up an image and videos can make that image come to life.' One of their most extreme was the video for 'I Want to Break Free'. The whole group dressed up in drag. Freddie himself wore a tight pink jumper, false breasts and a skimpy black mini skirt. The video features him vacuuming the floor of a suburban living room.

But Freddie Mercury's close friend, impresario Dave Clark, says the singer wasn't just larking about. 'When you look at a lot of his videos he knew just how to depict what was said in the lyrics.

He knew exactly what he wanted, right down to the look and the lighting of the whole thing.'

In 1978, Queen was recording in Nice. That year, the Tour de France – the world's greatest bicycle race – passed through Nice. And the athletic cyclists inspired Freddie to write 'Bicycle Race'. It was decided that it would be released as a double A-side with 'Fat Bottomed Girls', written by Brian May. And they arranged to hold a race of their own, with 65 naked women taking part, in a football stadium in London. The event was photographed for Queen publicity shots. But the band had to reckon with an unexpected expense. Halfords refused to take back the saddles that had been used in the race. And Queen's problems

weren't over then. The single was released with a rear photo of the winning
cyclist on the cover. But it caused such
outrage that each copy had to have black
panties painted on.

For their 'Miracle' video the band auditioned kids who looked like the four of
them had looked when they were kids.
Mercury's child double was dressed up
in his trademark leotard and black
leather jacket and strutted and pranced
about the stage in a very close imitation
of the singer himself. 'The resemblance
was quite frightening', Freddie said.

Over the Top

Sometimes Freddie's theatricality would go too far. The other members of the band would occasionally feel that Freddie had taken his flamboyance to a vulgar extreme. John Deacon once told an interviewer for *Rolling Stone* magazine: 'Some of us hate it. But that's Freddie and you can't stop it. Like one time he did an interview and said things like "We're dripping with money darling".' It may have been vulgar, but it was the truth.

Sometimes even the audiences felt that
Freddie had stepped over some bound-
ary into bad taste. At their huge concert
in Rio de Janerio in 1985, the band
played 'I Want to Break Free' in front
of 325,000 fans. And Freddie appeared
wearing the same costume he had worn
for the song's video – inflatable bosoms,
tight skirt and jumper and wig. The
crowd proceeded to pelt the band with
stones, cans and bottles. Freddie hadn't
realized that for South American audiences 'I Want to Break Free' was like a
hymn to freedom. It was a song they
cherished as symbolizing their desire to
break free from repressive political re-
gimes. So Freddie quickly ripped off his
wig and false boobs. Afterwards he joked
that another great queen had been
stoned once – the Queen of Sheba.

All members of the band wrote songs. But Freddie provided real leadership for the group. He was also often behind the dramatic changes of direction that the band took. Each time they came out with a new sound – the hard rock of a song like 'Tie Your Mother Down', the grinding disco sound of 'Another One Bites the Dust', a New Age sound like 'Radio Gaga' – they risked alienating their fans. But Freddie wasn't going to be pigeonholed. 'I like to deliberately do things that aren't considered Queen', he said. 'I always believe in doing something different. Otherwise what's the point? You might as well give out copies of your old records.'

Freddie was a perfectionist and a prima donna. One of the band's bodyguards

Freddie's house in Kensington

Freddie at one of his famous birthday parties

was given the job of pulling all the thorns off the dozens of roses that Freddie would throw out into the audience each night. Freddie said this was to prevent the crowd from getting hurt. But Pete the bodyguard says it was to save Freddie's delicate fingers.

Of course, Freddie had a musical career independently of Queen. Perhaps his most famous solo works were his collaborations with the Spanish opera singer Montserrat Caballé. Freddie had long been an opera lover, but he had always preferred the male voice. However, in May 1983 he went to a performance of Verdi's *Un Ballo in Maschera* at the Royal Opera House. Pavarotti was singing the male lead, and the female soloist was Caballé. Freddie was awestruck by the power and beauty of her voice. When the two later met at a lunch in the Barcelona Ritz, Freddie played the Spanish diva some of his music, and Caballé suggested they should record an album together. She also asked Freddie to write a song for her about her home city. That song became the world-famous 'Barcelona'. The single was chosen as the official theme tune for the 1992 Barcelona Olympics. Working with Caballé was one of the most fulfilling experiences of Freddie's musical career. After their album had been put together Freddie said simply, 'What else is there left for me to do?'

Sex and Drugs and Partying

Off-stage, Freddie's life was as over-the-top as the singer on stage. He told one reporter: 'Excess is part of my nature. To me dullness is a disease.' His sex life was, to say the least, active. He once confessed to having an enormous sex drive. 'I'll go to bed with anything,' he boasted. 'And my bed is so huge it can comfortably sleep six. I prefer my sex without any involvement. There are times when I just live for sex.' He bedded a procession of men that he met in gay clubs where he'd go to live it up after a gig. Of course, because he was Freddie Mercury, he was never short of willing sexual partners.

Freddie's partying was legendary. The rock world is no stranger to extravagant parties, but Freddie's were even more extravagant then most. It became standard for Queen to throw parties after their concerts, and those were spectacular affairs. However, the real knees-ups were Freddie's birthday bashes. It was quite standard for him to splash out £50,000 on drink and entertainments. One party reputedly cost £200,000 with £30,000 going just on champagne. Drugs featured heavily, especially cocaine. Reportedly, he and his guests snorted £24,000-worth of the white powder at one of his parties. Freddie loved to hold parties because he liked to make others happy.

At a famous 'hat party' in Kensington a fabulous range of millinery was on display. But Freddie outdid everyone with an enormously tall top hat, one of ten that he'd had made especially. When he pulled a little string, the top of the hat would open, and a huge artificial penis would pop out.

One of the most notorious parties was held at the Roof Top Gardens in London following a Queen concert in 1986. The waiters and waitresses at the party appeared to be wearing incredibly skin-tight uniforms – until the guests looked closer and realized that they were actually naked. Their bodies had been painted to look as though they were dressed. It took five hours for each person to be painted. Former topless model Sam Fox was among the celebrities present at that bash. As the party reached its climax, she and Freddie leapt up on a makeshift stage to sing a surprise duet.

Freddie's 40th birthday party was an outrageous affair held in Munich. He told all the male guests to come in drag. But he turned up in a parody of gentlemanly elegance – a Bavarian military jacket glittering with medals, and trousers covered with huge diamond shapes. He had the party filmed, because he wanted to use the footage for the

Freddie with one of his beloved cats

Freddie's close friend Mary Austin

upcoming video to his fourth solo single, 'Living on My Own'. But among the 300 guests were various top cats in the recording industry as well as numerous business wheeler-dealers. Many of them were caught on film doing things they didn't want publicized. In the end the video was scrapped, allegedly because the record company feared it would cause offence. It wasn't clear if it was the audience or the participants who would have been offended. Afterwards, Mercury said: 'It was a great do. I had to have something lavish to face up to the thought of being forty! It was great that everyone entered into the spirit of the thing.'

His 41st party was held at the ultra-exclusive Pykes hotel on the island of

Ibiza off the coast of Spain. Ibiza became infamous for its partying lifestyle in the 1980s. Europe's young and fashionable would descend on the island for weekends of sex, drugs and music. And when Freddie was on the island, the sex, drugs and music were more excessive than ever. For this birthday party, he hired a DC-9 jet to fly his friends in from England. The plane only just made it onto the island in one piece. Engine failure meant that the pilot had to bring the plane in on just one engine. But that didn't stop the party from being a huge success. It went on all night, and many of the guests never went to bed – they just climbed back on the plane the next day. Altogether 500 guests were invited. A huge firework display blazed Freddie's name over the Mediterranean sky, and he was treated to a 20-foot birthday cake.

He even managed to have an outrageous time at other people's parties. At a Royal Ballet gala he met Prince Andrew, who fished Freddie's white silk scarf out of a drink and wrung it out for him. When the Prince asked Freddie to sing him a song, the singer said he would – if the Queen's son would swing from the chandelier's first. Sadly, the Prince refused. He also turned down Freddie's invitation to accompany him and a group of Royal Ballet dancers to the gay nightclub Heaven.

Even when he wasn't on stage, Freddie was performing. One evening Freddie and his assistant Joe Fanelli went to see a performance of the musical *Time*, for which Freddie had written a track. As the first half of the show came to an end, Freddie decided he wanted to sell ice creams during the interval. 'I did try to point out that it wasn't one of his better ideas', says Joe. 'Especially since he wouldn't have a clue what a pound coin looked like, so how on earth was he going to make sure the people paid the right price and were given the correct change?' Freddie's solution to that problem was to buy up the whole supply of ice creams and then give them away. So he put on the white coat and began handing out the ice creams. But he soon got bored of that, so he began chucking the ice creams into the crowd. 'He was hurling ice lollies and tubs and Cornettos

Floral tributes after Freddie's death

Roses from Elton John

all over the place', Joe remembers. 'They were landing in people's laps, on their heads, it was chaos. Some people even threw them back!'

He Stoops to Shop

Freddie was a certified shopaholic. He once said, 'I love to spend, spend, spend. After all, that's what money is there for.' The group's tours to Japan provided him with an opportunity to indulge his fetish for shopping. He would buy beautiful silks and armfuls of kimonos. He also built up a fabulous collection of Japanese art. And later he would make lightning trips to Japan just to go shopping. On one of those he spent £25,000 on

antiques and art. During one of his
shopping sprees in Tokyo, one of the
city's biggest stores, the Shibuya Seibu,
closed whole floors so Freddie could
have a completely personal service. Another time he spent hundreds of thousands of pounds on a 144-piece dinner
service handpainted with miniature copies of Constable paintings. Each serving
plate cost £20,000. He spent £50,000
just on fish. He bought hugely expensive
Japanese koi carp to fill the pond at his
Kensington home. Exclusive jewellers
Cartier would stay open after hours so
Freddie could shop for precious stones
and gold without being bothered. 'I
believe in being extravagant', he said.
'Sometimes all I want from life is to
make pots of money and then go off
and spend it.' He himself rarely carried

money – like the real Queen, he would joke. He entrusted his cash and credit cards to the friends and assistants who would trail after him on his shopping trips. For them, it was an exhausting experience. Joe Fanelli said, 'Shopping with Freddie is like hitting yourself on the head repeatedly with an ice pick – it feels so good when you stop.' Freddie once said – only half joking – that when he died he wanted to be buried like a Pharaoh, surrounded by all his fabulous belongings.

He was passionate about fine art. He amassed a collection that was among the best private collections in Britain. He bought Impressionist paintings, Japanese wood-cuts, and works by Victorian masters. One of his favourite artists was the Russian painter Marc Chagall. According to publicist Roxy Meade, 'Freddie had exquisite taste. It was never tacky like so many showbusiness stars.'

His Kensington home was another of his great and costly luxuries. He bought it for £500,000 – in cash. He was later offered a million pounds for it, but refused to sell. He said he'd always wanted to own a mansion and that's what it was. It had eight bedrooms, four marble bathrooms, a jacuzzi and a minstrels' gallery. But Freddie's bedroom was the most special room in the house. It was his inner sanctum, and his love nest. It was created by knocking together three of the original rooms. It had a colonnade of Romanesque columns and an emperor-sized bed – which had to be hoisted up to the top floor of the house by a crane. Above the bed was a system of lights controlled from a complicated electronic console. With it, Freddie could create a mood to fit his own: dawn light, sunset, a romantic dusk. One of the bathrooms was fitted out in black marble shot through with gold, another in orange marble. The refurbishing of the house took years. But when it was finally ready, Freddie decided to move in for a weekend to see how it felt. He never moved out. And he brought with him his beloved cats, Oscar and Tiffany. The Kensington house would become a sanctuary for Freddie towards the end of his life, as he put his days of wild partying and high living behind him.

The Other Freddie Mercury

Although Freddie is remembered as the camp and over-the-top frontman for Queen, there was another side to him. Inside the showman there was a troubled and lonely man. It's no surprise that one of his greatest solo hits was a cover of 'The Great Pretender'.

Many of his friends would say that his wild, gay lifestyle was only one superficial aspect of his life. His longest intimate relationship was not with a man, but a woman – Mary Austin. She was a solid rock that he could cling to in the storm of his one-night stands and troubled relationships. He met her when she was working at the trendy 1960s boutique Biba, in Freddie's old stomping ground, Kensington. But he was shy about asking her for a date. 'It took him nearly six months to finally ask me out', she remembers. 'I thought he fancied my best friend, so I used to avoid him. One night we were at one of his gigs, and after it had finished he came looking for me. I left him at the bar with my friend to go to the loo, but actually I sneaked out. He was furious!' But eventually he drummed up the courage to ask her out, and she became a constant companion. They lived together for

seven years, and even after he began to
live a gay life, Mary Austin remained his
confidante, and a shoulder for him to cry
on. After he moved out, he bought her
an apartment minutes away from his
own so they could be in constant con-
tact. And when Mary gave birth to her
first child, Freddie became the boy's
godfather. As well as being there when
Freddie needed advice or comfort, Mary
would help the star get ready for his
shows, even doing his make-up for him.
In fact, many credit Mary with helping
to create Freddie Mercury, the glitzy
showman with the outrageous clothes
and posturing style.

Although Freddie never announced to
the world that he was gay, he lived a life
of promiscuous homosexuality. But he

would oscillate between one-night stands and prolonged, domesticated relationships. He often said that his promiscuity was a way of hiding from his loneliness. He loved being in love. And when he was, he would be inspired, churning out songs and music. He could live a very quiet life when he wanted to, tending to his garden and entertaining friends at home instead of rushing out to go partying. Close friends say they believe he wished he could have had a family. Others say he never really recovered from the shock of leaving exotic Bombay for Feltham.

And Freddie was not a typical rock star. Friends remember him as being caring and considerate. On one occasion, Freddie heard about a young fan who was in a coma following a car accident. Colin was only 25, and considered himself a Freddie lookalike. The Queen singer wrote a song especially for him called 'Keep on Smiling', which he recorded and sent to the young fan. Sadly, Colin never came out of his coma. When he died, the tape of 'Keep on Smiling' was buried with him. On other occasions Freddie would send money anonymously to people whose tragedies touched him. And he was terribly fond of his animals. When one of his cats died after an unsuccessful operation, he flew straight home from Munich for the funeral. He broke down in tears again when one of his beloved carp died.

Freddie could also be very shy for such

an apparent extrovert. On one occasion, he agreed to put on a surprise performance at the birthday party of one of his friends' sons. But he almost couldn't go out in front of the kids because he was struck with stage fright.

The King of Queen is Dead

By 1986, Freddie had abandoned his life of excess. He wouldn't admit to the world that he had AIDS. But people were beginning to suspect that something was wrong. That year, he said he was sick of touring. 'I don't think a forty-two-year-old man should be running about in a leotard any more', he declared. 'It's not very becoming.' But the truth was that Freddie knew he was dying. He no longer had the strength to strut about the stage as though he was an immortal who would live forever.

His appearance in public became rarer and rarer as he became a recluse in his Kensington home. When he went into the studio to record 'I'm Going Slightly Mad', it was obvious to the crew that Freddie was very ill. The technicians were told that he would tire easily, but AIDS was never mentioned. Instead, they were told that he'd hurt his knee. He would have to wear thick make-up to conceal the blotches that the disease had left on his face. And under his suit he wore a thick T-shirt to disguise how emaciated his body had become.

Freddie even kept the terrible secret of his illness from the other members of

Queen. And it was only 24 hours before the end that the dying singer admitted to the world that he had AIDS. He released a short statement: 'I wish to confirm that I have been tested HIV positive and have AIDS. I felt it correct to keep this information private to date in order to protect the intimacy of those around me. However, the time has now come for my friends and fans around the world to know the truth. I hope everyone will join with me, my doctors and all those worldwide in the fight against this terrible disease.'

When the end came, it was unexpected. He died so quickly that his parents didn't even have time to get to his bedside. At 7 p.m. on the bitterly cold evening of Sunday 24 November 1991 Freddie

Mercury's reign as the king of Queen
came to an end. He was just 45 years old,
tragic proof that the candle that burns
twice as bright burns half as long.

His funeral was a small, private affair –
except that it took four Daimler hearses
just to carry the flowers. The service was
conducted in the Zoroastrian faith.

Post Mortem

There were those who said that Freddie should have owned up to having AIDS earlier. They argued that he could have removed some of the stigma of the disease if he had been honest about it. And like the basketball hero Magic Johnson, he could have spread the word about the need for safe sex and used his fame to raise money for AIDS research.

But he did contribute to the AIDS cause after his death. The three remaining members of Queen decided to re-release Freddie's first great hit, 'Bohemian Rhapsody', and donate the proceeds to the Terrence Higgins Trust, the British AIDS charity. The profits from sales in America would go to the foundation set up by Magic Johnson. The single went back to number 1, sixteen years after it first took the chart's top spot. In the first six days after it was released, the single sold over 100,000 copies in the UK alone and went on to sell over 1.1 million copies. So the song that launched Freddie into superstardom was the theme tune to his death. But the last single that Queen released before Freddie died was 'The Show

Must Go On'. The show may go on, but without the world's greatest rock showman, it'll be tamer and less exotic affair.